# PLAIN
### and
### not
### so
# PLAIN

# ACADEMY

**A simpler approach to home based schooling**

# Summer review

of

# First Grade

# Basic Skills

This book is for the home educator or anyone looking to improve upon their child's skill sets. It contains multiple lessons and skills that will help reinforce your first graders knowledge before they enter second grade. It reviews math concepts, reading concepts, and various grammar lessons.

How do I recommend you do this book? However you feel is comfortable. Let me share with you how I wrote the book and will intend to use it with my children.

On page 7, there is a suggestion on how to keep track of your child's book reading this summer. I would recommend doing this to encourage more reading.

The next few pages all have to do with word lists that are helpful for your child to know. I would start with one and work through it until your child can say them without assistance. Mark off the completed box and then move on. Do this daily before you start worksheet lessons on page 25.

I would then suggest you do three pages of learning per day in addition to the word lists. Beginning on page 25.

Included are enough pages to do 64 days of extra work.

I hope you find this resource helpful in your child's academic growth. My intention is to help simplify learning to create a more peaceful, organized, and happy home.

Be blessed,

Amy Maryon

founder and owner of www.plainandnotsoplain.com a simpler lifestyle in our complex world

**Motivate your student to read this summer by creating a caterpillar.**

To create this display, cut a supply of large construction paper circles. Add pom-pom eyes, a yarn mouth, and pipe cleaner antennae to one circle to resemble a caterpillar's head.  Attach the caterpillar's head on the wall.  Tell your student that for every book they read, a segment will be added to the caterpillar.  The student must write their name (if you have multiple readers), the book title, and the author's name on a construction paper circle.

Your student will be amazed at how long their caterpillar grows by the end of summer time.

# SHORT VOWEL

| short a | short e | short i |
|---------|---------|---------|
| add | bed | big |
| bad | beg | bill |
| bag | desk | crib |
| bat | egg | dish |
| cab | fed | fib |
| cap | fence | grin |
| dad | get | hill |
| fan | help | in |
| fat | jet | king |
| ham | leg | lid |
| hat | met | milk |
| jam | nest | pig |
| man | pet | rip |
| map | red | ship |
| nap | sent | six |
| pan | ten | this |
| rag | test | tin |
| ran | vet | whip |
| sad | web | win |
| tag | yes | zip |

| completed | completed | completed |

| short o | short u |
|---------|---------|
| box | bug |
| cot | bus |
| dog | cub |
| drop | cup |
| fog | drum |
| fox | fun |
| hop | gum |
| hot | hut |
| jot | jug |
| knob | luck |
| lock | mud |
| mom | mug |
| mop | nut |
| not | pup |
| on | rug |
| pot | run |
| rock | sun |
| song | tub |
| top | umbrella |
| loss | up |

| completed | completed |

# LONG VOWEL

| long a | long e | long i |
|--------|--------|--------|
| ape | bee | bite |
| bake | cheese | bride |
| cape | deep | fire |
| cave | feet | five |
| date | free | hive |
| face | he | ice |
| flame | heat | kite |
| gate | key | life |
| grape | knee | line |
| hate | lead | mice |
| lake | meet | mine |
| make | pea | nice |
| name | please | nine |
| page | read | pine |
| plane | see | ripe |
| rake | she | size |
| same | three | smile |
| skate | tree | time |
| take | we | vine |
| tape | week | wide |

| completed | completed | completed |

| long o | long u |
|--------|--------|
| bone | cube |
| close | cute |
| cone | fume |
| dose | fuse |
| froze | huge |
| globe | human |
| hole | humor |
| home | mule |
| joke | music |
| lobe | mute |
| mole | tube |
| nose | tulip |
| note | tune |
| pole | unicorn |
| robe | unicycle |
| stove | uniform |
| tote | unit |
| vote | use |
| woke | useful |
|  | yule |

completed

completed

# CONSONANT BLENDS AND DIGRAPHS

## bl
black
blame
blank
blast
bleed
blend
blind
blink
block
blow
blue
blush

completed

## br
brag
brain
brake
brand
brave
breeze
brick
bring
broke
broom
brother
brown
brush

completed

## ch
chain
chair
chalk
chance
change
chase
chat
check
cheek
chest
chick
chin
choose
chop

completed

## cl
clam
clap
class
claw
clay
clean
climb
clock
close
clown

completed

## cr
crab
crack
crash
creep
crib
crime
crop
cross
crow

completed

## dr
drag
draw
dream
dress
drip
drum
dry

completed

## fl

flag
flake
flame
flap
flash
flat
flip
float
flow
fly

completed

## fr

frame
free
freeze
fresh
friend
frog
from
front
fry

completed

## gl

glad
glass
glove
glow
glue

completed

## gr

grab
grape
grass
green
grin
grip
grow

completed

## pl

place
plan
plane
plate
play
please
plot
plug
plus

completed

## sh

shade
share
shark
she
sheep
sheet
shell
shine
ship
shirt
shop
shot
should
show
shut

completed

| **pr** |
|---|
| press |
| price |
| pride |
| prince |
| prize |

completed

| **sl** |
|---|
| slam |
| sled |
| sleep |
| slid |
| slip |
| slow |

completed

| **sm** |
|---|
| small |
| smart |
| smell |
| smile |
| smoke |

completed

| **st** |
|---|
| stand |
| step |
| sting |
| stop |
| store |
| street |

completed

| **th** |
|---|
| that |
| the |
| then |
| these |
| they |
| thin |
| think |
| this |
| thumb |

completed

| **wh** |
|---|
| whale |
| what |
| when |
| where |
| white |
| why |

completed

# COMPOUND WORDS

| | | |
|---|---|---|
| airplane | cupcake | goldfish |
| barnyard | daydream | grandparents |
| baseball | daylight | grasshopper |
| bathtub | doghouse | groundhog |
| bedroom | dollhouse | hairbrush |
| beehive | doorbell | haircut |
| birdbath | downstairs | handshake |
| birdhouse | fingernail | homework |
| butterfly | firecracker | indoor |
| chalkboard | flashlight | keyboard |
| cowboy | football | ladybug |

| completed | completed | completed |
|---|---|---|

| | | |
|---|---|---|
| lighthouse | policeman | snowman |
| mailbox | popcorn | somebody |
| newspaper | railroad | something |
| nobody | rainbow | strawberry |
| notebook | sailboat | suitcase |
| outside | sandpaper | sunlight |
| paintbrush | scarecrow | sunshine |
| pancake | seahorse | teamwork |
| patchwork | sidewalk | teapot |
| peanut | skateboard | toothbrush |
| playground | snowflake | underline |
| | | watermelon |
| | | weekend |

| completed | completed | completed |
|---|---|---|

Grab some small objects like beans or seeds and place a couple in the squares and add them up.

_____ + _____ = _____          _____ + _____ = _____

_____ + _____ = _____          _____ + _____ = _____

_____ + _____ = _____          _____ + _____ = _____

Choose an antonym for the words given below.  Antonym means opposite.

above      _____

alike      _____

always      _____

asleep      _____

attack      _____

back      _____

beautiful      _____

before      _____

begin      _____

best      _____

Practice writing your letters correctly.

A

a

B

b

C

c

1

2

3

4

Write your name—two times

|  |  |  |  |  |
| --- | --- | --- | --- | --- |
|  |  |  |  |  |
|  |  |  |  |  |
|  |  |  |  |  |
|  |  |  |  |  |
|  |  |  |  |  |
|  |  |  |  |  |
|  |  |  |  |  |
|  |  |  |  |  |
|  |  |  |  |  |
|  |  |  |  |  |
|  |  |  |  |  |
|  |  |  |  |  |
|  |  |  |  |  |
|  |  |  |  |  |
|  |  |  |  |  |
|  |  |  |  |  |

Students will enjoy this activity.  Give them a small bag of Jelly beans or multi colored fruit candies.  Help them create a simple graph with the various color candies.  Have your student sort the candies by color;  then have them count and graph each amount.  Conclude the activity with a treat---eating a sampling of the candies!

At the bottom of the graph, write the names of the colors or color in with crayons.

Choose an antonym for the words given below. Antonym means opposite.

big        _____

bottom     _____

bright      _____

clean       _____

close       _____

cold        _____

crooked    _____

dark        _____

day         _____

deep        _____

Practice writing your letters correctly.

D

d

E

e

F

f

5

6

7

8

Write your name—and your pet's name

For this math activity take a piece of paper and cut it evenly into 4 sections. Write the numbers 1-4 on the squares. Do this on multiple pieces of paper up to the number 24. Place the squares on the floor in order, in a circle pattern for your student.

Game suggestions:

- Call out a number and have them stand by it.
- Play some music and when the music stops, have them tell you which number they are standing on.
- Practice skip counting by stepping on every other number as they are calling them out loud.
- You can place them in a straight line and have them practice counting by 3's, 5's etc by stepping by the numbers.
- Play number mix up and put the numbers in a pile and let your child put them in the correct order.

Keep these numbers as they will do more activities another day.

Choose an antonym for the words given below.  Antonym means opposite.

difficult      _____

down          _____

dry             _____

early           _____

easy            _____

empty         _____

evil             _____

far              _____

fast            _____

first           _____

# Practice writing your letters correctly.

G

g

H

h

I

i

9

10

11

12

Write your favorite color and favorite animal

Grab a handful of small objects such as dry beans, popcorn seeds, toothpicks, or counting blocks.  Ask your child the following:

Estimate how many there are?_____

Now count them.  How many are there actually?_____

Were you close in estimation?   yes  or no

---------------------------------------------------------------------------------------------------------

Think about all of the chairs that we have in our home.

Do you think there are fewer than 10? Yes or no

Now count them.  How many are there actually?_____

Were you close in estimation?  Yes or no

---------------------------------------------------------------------------------------------

Would it take more than 10 steps to get the bathroom?  Yes or no

Now count them.  How many steps does it take?

Were you correct?  Yes or no

Do we have more than 50 windows in our home? Yes or no

Now count them.  How many are there actually?_____

Were you correct? Yes or no

Choose an antonym for the words given below. Antonym means opposite.

forget     _____

give     _____

happy     _____

hard     _____

healthy     _____

heavy     _____

high     _____

kind     _____

large     _____

leave     _____

Practice writing your letters correctly.

J                          j

K                          k

L                          l

13                         14

15                         16

List three things you like to do in the summer:

1

2

3

# Estimation

Can you hold more than 25 pennies in your hand? Yes or no

Now do it.  Were you correct? Yes or no

-------------------------------------------------------------------------------------

Would it take more than 30 steps to get to your bedroom? Yes or no

Now do it.  How many does it actually take?_____

Was that MORE or LESS than 30?

-------------------------------------------------------------------------------------

Are there more than 50 books in our home? Yes or no

Count them.  How many do we actually have?_____

Was that MORE or LESS than 50?

-------------------------------------------------------------------------------------

Can you hold 20 pieces of silverware in your hands? Yes or no

Try it.  Can you do it? Yes or no

-------------------------------------------------------------------------------------

Do we have more than 10 lights in our home? Yes or no

Now count them.  How many do we actually have?

Was that MORE or LESS than 10?

Choose an antonym for the words given below.  Antonym means opposite.

long          _____

loose         _____

lose          _____

many          _____

noisy         _____

on            _____

polite        _____

pull          _____

rich          _____

rough         _____

# Practice writing your letters correctly.

M                                           m

N                                           n

O                                           o

17                                    18

19                                    20

List three fruits you like to eat:

1

2

3

Fill a small bag full of popped popcorn, dry crackers, pretzels, or dry cereal.

How many pieces do you think are in this bag?_____

Have your child eat one piece at a time and have them make tally marks on this paper to keep track of the pieces.

For example: ‖‖‖ this means 5. ‖‖ this means 3

| Tally marks |
| --- |
| |

Determine how many pieces were in the bag. Write that number here _____.

Compare that to the number you estimated earlier. Were you close? yes or no

Choose an antonym for the words given below.  Antonym means opposite.

save        _____

short       _____

start       _____

strong      _____

tame        _____

thick       _____

true        _____

wide        _____

yes         _____

Practice writing your letters correctly.

P                                          p

Q                                          q

R                                          r

21                                     22

23                                     24

List three vegetables you like to eat:

1

2

3

Place a handful of small objects inside of a cloth bag. You can use any small toys or objects.

Give the bag to your child and let them feel inside of the bag for a few seconds.

Estimate about how many objects are in that bag?

_____

Count the actual number of objects:_____

Were you close to estimating? Yes or no

Fill the bag again with other objects and ask the same questions.

Estimate about how many objects are in that bag?

_____

Count the actual number of objects:_____

Were you close to estimating? Yes or no

Fill the bag again with other objects and ask the same questions.

Estimate about how many objects are in that bag?

_____

Count the actual number of objects:_____

Were you close to estimating? Yes or no

Practice initial sounds.  Look at this letter, what sound does it make?

Now draw five objects that begin with this letter that you would like to find in a treasure box. Label the objects as well.

a

Practice writing your letters correctly.

S

T

U

s

t

u

25

27

26

28

Write your full name:

Write your birthday:

For this math activity take a piece of paper and cut it evenly into 4 sections. Write the numbers 1-4 on the squares. Do this on multiple pieces of paper up to the number 24. Place the squares on the floor in order, in a circle pattern for your student.

Game suggestions:

- Call out a number and have them stand by it.
- Play some music and when the music stops, have them tell you which number they are standing on.
- Practice skip counting by stepping on every other number as they are calling them out loud.
- You can place them in a straight line and have them practice counting by 3's, 5's etc by stepping by the numbers.
- Play number mix up and put the numbers in a pile and let your child put them in the correct order.

Keep these numbers as they will do more activities another day.

Practice initial sounds.  Look at this letter, what sound does it make?

Now draw five objects that begin with this letter that you would like to find in a treasure box. Label the objects as well.

b

Practice writing your letters correctly.

V

V

W

W

X

X

29

30

31

32

List three things you like to do in the water:

1

2

3

Draw the word problem in pictures to help solve.

Mom ate 8 cherries for breakfast this morning.  At lunchtime she ate 5 more. How many cherries did Mom eat?_____

Madelyn had 5 baby dolls to play with.  Autumn brought 3 more to play together with.  How many baby dolls did they have in all?_____

Jentzen had 4 train cars to add to his track. Collin gave him3 more. How many train cars did Jentzen have altogether?_____

Stephen built a block tower.  He started out with 6 blocks. He carefully added 2 more before it fell.  How tall was his tower before it  fell?_____

Practice initial sounds.  Look at this letter, what sound does it make?

Now draw five objects that begin with this letter that you would like to find in a treasure box. Label the objects as well.

# C

Practice writing your letters correctly.

Y

y

Z

z

33

34

35

36

List three things you like to do in the wintertime:

1

2

3

Draw pictures to help solve the problems.

Our cat had 10 kittens.  We gave away 6 of the kittens to friends. How many kittens do we have left?_____

I had a bag full of candy bars.  I started out with 10 candy bars.  I gave each of my 5 children a candy bar.  How many do I have left?_____

Brooklyn baked a dozen cupcakes.  Her friends ate 5 of them.  How many does she have left?_____

I want to give all my children a caramel covered apple for a treat.  I have 8 children. I made 3 apples already. How many more do I still have to make?_____

Practice initial sounds.  Look at this letter, what sound does it make?

Now draw five objects that begin with this letter that you would like to find in a treasure box. Label the objects as well.

d

Ask your child to imagine that they are a form of transportation, such as a helicopter, a sailboat, or a bus. Encourage the child to imagine their life as the vehicle. Have them think about what they would do all day, what they would eat, and whom they would meet. Next have them write and illustrate a story titled "My day as a (vehicle)." Let them share with the family when it is complete. Draw a picture below and write a title on the first line.

Let your child practice using a calculator.

Have your student write their seven digit telephone number on the line. Instruct them to find the sum of their phone number by adding all seven digits. Do this with multiple numbers of people that you know. Write the person's name on the first line.


(my)_____number

_____total equals_____


_____number

_____total equals_____


_____number

_____total equals_____


_____number

_____total equals_____


Whose phone number has the largest sum?_____

Practice initial sounds.  Look at this letter, what sound does it make?

Now draw five objects that begin with this letter that you would like to find in a treasure box. Label the objects as well.

e

Help your child write an Acrostic with the letters of their name. Write their name vertical down the side of this paper and write words that describe them after each letter.  For example: A-awesome M-mindful Y-young

Calculator fun. Have your child choose which foods they would eat for a meal. Write down the foods they would eat and how much it would cost total using a calculator. Ask another friend what their choices would be and see whose meal would cost more.

| Pizza | fries | burger | grill cheese | ice cream | drink |
|-------|-------|--------|--------------|-----------|-------|
| $1.25 | $1.00 | $3.00 | $2.50 | $1.75 | $1.00 |

The meal I would choose includes:

1

2

3

The total amount equals:_____

The meal my friend would choose includes:

1

2

3

The total amount equals:_____

Practice initial sounds.  Look at this letter, what sound does it make?

Now draw five objects that begin with this letter that you would like to find in a treasure box. Label the objects as well.

f

Draw a picture of your family doing an activity.  Write the activity that your family enjoys doing together at the bottom.

My family enjoys

# Estimation math

Fill a clear, plastic jar with items for students to count.  Items such as macaroni, peanuts, dried beans, buttons, etc.  Ask each student how many items they would estimate are in the jar.  Write the number on this page, along with other student's guesses.

_____

_____

_____

_____

_____

## Circle the HIGHEST and the LOWEST guess.

Then count together the items in the jar as your student's clap their hands.

Write the actual number of objects _____

Practice initial sounds.  Look at this letter, what sound does it make?

Now draw five objects that begin with this letter that you would like to find in a treasure box. Label the objects as well.

g

Create a flip book for your student.

To make a booklet, stack three, 8 ½"x11" sheets of white paper and hold the pages vertically in front of you. Slide the top sheet upward one inch; then repeat the process for the second sheet. Next fold the paper thicknesses forward to create six graduated layers or pages. Staple close to the fold.

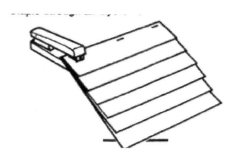

Have your child create their own story. Do they need help? On the first page they can write: I have a dog name Ruby. (then draw a picture of them and their dog). Next page, He loves to go for walks. (then draw a picture of taking him for a walk) Third page, He sleeps at the foot of my bed. (picture of dog sleeping by bed) Fourth page, He barks at strangers (image of dog barking) Fifth page, He is the best dog in the world. (image of hugging the dog).

They can write about what they like to do in the summer.

All about their pet.

What they did on vacation.

Fill in the chart with tally marks and the correct number of objects in their home. When finished marking with tally marks, have them write the number on the line.

| Doors | Couches | Beds |
|---|---|---|
| _____ | _____ | _____ |
| **Windows** | **Dolls** | **Vehicles** |
| _____ | _____ | _____ |
| **People** | **Plates** | **Tables** |
| _____ | _____ | _____ |
| **Fans** | **Rugs** | **Hair brushes** |
| _____ | _____ | _____ |
| **Tooth brushes** | **Fireplaces** | **Swings** |
| _____ | _____ | _____ |

Practice initial sounds.  Look at this letter, what sound does it make?

Now draw five objects that begin with this letter that you would like to find in a treasure box. Label the objects as well.

h

# Pop up cards

Students will enjoy illustrating their stories in a pop-up card.   Have your student publish their favorite story in a self-made pop-up card.

To make a pop-up card:

1.   Fold in half a 9"x12" sheet of white construction paper.
2.   Cut two 2-inch slits in the center of the fold about 1 ½ inches apart.  Open the card and write a short story near the bottom of it.
3.   Illustrate the main character in the story on a three-inch square of construction paper. Cut out the illustration.
4.   Pull the narrow strip in the center of the opened card forward and crease it in the opposite direction from the fold.  Glue the cutout to the lower half of the strip;  then illustrate the inside of the card as desired.
5.   Close the card, making sure the strip stays inside.
6.   To complete the project, write the title of the store on the outside of the card.

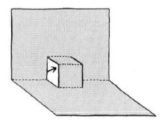

A sample story may include:

One day I was walking in the forest when I met a bear named Susan.  We became friends. I took her food and taught her how to dance.

Make a bear and attach it to the square.  Color in the background to look like a forest.

Reinforce graphing skills with a tasty treat. Give each student a snack sized bag of color candies. Have each child sort and graph their candies by color on their graph paper. Then using the corresponding crayon color, have them color one square for each candy of that color. Encourage them to write the total number of each color on the graph. Then challenge the child to add the total number of candies.

| | | | | | |
|---|---|---|---|---|---|
| | | | | | |
| | | | | | |
| | | | | | |
| | | | | | |
| | | | | | |
| | | | | | |
| | | | | | |
| | | | | | |
| | | | | | |

Practice initial sounds.  Look at this letter, what sound does it make?

Now draw five objects that begin with this letter that you would like to find in a treasure box. Label the objects as well.

i

What month is your birthday? _____

What is your favorite dessert?_____

Are you **left-handed** or **right-handed**? Circle the correct one.

What is your favorite color?_____

How many letters are in your first name?_____

Are you a boy or a girl? _____

How many pockets do you have?_____

Would you rather have a **hot dog** or a **burger**? Circle the correct one.

How many pets do you have?_____

How many teeth have you lost?_____

What is your favorite flavor of ice cream?_____

Nonstandard measuring

Have student trace their hand out of construction paper and cut out.  They will be using this to measure objects with.

How many hands long is the table?_____

How many hands tall is the door?_____

How many hands wide is the window?_____

How many hands tall is the refrigerator?_____

How many hands tall are you?_____

Talk to your child about how this answer may be different when using other people's hands sizes.  Lead them to the conclusion that the measurements may be different because everyone's hands are different sizes.

Practice initial sounds.  Look at this letter, what sound does it make?

Now draw five objects that begin with this letter that you would like to find in a treasure box. Label the objects as well.

j

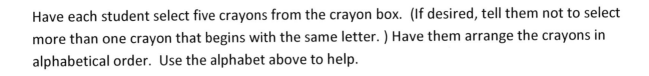

Have each student select five crayons from the crayon box. (If desired, tell them not to select more than one crayon that begins with the same letter. ) Have them arrange the crayons in alphabetical order. Use the alphabet above to help.

Write down the names of the people in your family on scrap pieces of paper. Have your child put them in ABC order.

Have your child draw four toys that have different beginning sounds on scrap pieces of paper. Have them place them in ABC order in front of them.

Yarn measurement.  Cut a length of yarn and let your child measure the following:

How far they can do a somersault?_____

How far they can take a giant step?_____

How tall they are?_____

How tall the door is?_____

How long the hallway is?_____

How long the vehicle is?_____

Practice initial sounds.  Look at this letter, what sound does it make?

Now draw five objects that begin with this letter that you would like to find in a treasure box. Label the objects as well.

k

Fill in the following chart with words that begin with something in your home. For each letter, have students name an item that begins with that sound.

## ABC's in our Home

| | | | |
|---|---|---|---|
| A | | N | |
| B | | O | |
| C | | P | |
| D | | Q | |
| E | | R | |
| F | | S | |
| G | | T | |
| H | | U | |
| I | | V | |
| J | | W | |
| K | | X | |
| L | | Y | |
| M | | Z | |

Measuring

Hand your student a piece of spaghetti.   Let them measure the following:

My room is _____spaghetti lengths long.

My vehicle is _____spaghetti lengths long.

My body is _____spaghetti lengths tall.

My mom's body is_____spaghetti lengths tall.

My door is _____spaghtetti lengths tall.

Practice initial sounds.  Look at this letter, what sound does it make?

Now draw five objects that begin with this letter that you would like to find in a treasure box. Label the objects as well.

I

Read the following words to your student. If they hear a short sound "a" as in the word cat, then have them give a thumbs up. If they hear a long sound "a" as in sale, then have them give a thumbs down.

add

bad

bag

ape

bake

bat

cape

cap

face

jam

grape

make

sad

plane

rake

tape

# Shapes review

Have your child find you two of the following shapes in objects around the home.

rectangle

square

circle

triangle

oval

Practice initial sounds.  Look at this letter, what sound does it make?

Now draw five objects that begin with this letter that you would like to find in a treasure box. Label the objects as well.

Read the following words to your student. If they hear a short sound "i" as in the word pig, then have them give a thumbs up. If they hear a long sound "i" as in word sign, then have them give a thumbs down.

big

crib

bite

fight

lid

five

mice

mine

nine

zip

whip

win

size

smile

six

in

**Which comes next in the pattern below:**

○ ○ ☆ ○ ○ ☆ ○ _____

AB  AB  AB  A _____

321  321  3_____

Pattern snack

Put your child's patterning and cooking skills together in a tasty way.  Use cubes of cheese, and small fruit such as grapes, strawberries, cut up watermelon, and bananas.  Have your child put the fruit and cheese in a pattern on the skewer.

Try and see if your child can guess which piece will come next in your pattern.

Practice initial sounds.  Look at this letter, what sound does it make?

Now draw five objects that begin with this letter that you would like to find in a treasure box. Label the objects as well.

n

Read the following words to your student. If they hear a short sound "E" as in the word bed, then have them give a thumbs up. If they hear a long sound "e" as in bee, then have them give a thumbs down.

beg

desk

fed

cheese

deep

sent

heat

nest

red

lead

meet

yes

web

see

she

three

# Draw me the following shapes:

| circle | square | rectangle |
|---|---|---|
| star | oval | pentagon |
| hexagon | diamond | cone |

Practice initial sounds.  Look at this letter, what sound does it make?

Now draw five objects that begin with this letter that you would like to find in a treasure box. Label the objects as well.

O

Read the following words to your student.  If they hear a short sound "o" as in the word cot, then have them give a thumbs up. If they hear a long sound "o" as in rope, then have them give a thumbs down.

box

fox

dog

bone

froze

hole

pot

top

nose

note

pole

mom

mop

hot

vote

Grab a crayon box and fill in each row in a pattern that your student chooses.

Practice initial sounds.  Look at this letter, what sound does it make?

Now draw five objects that begin with this letter that you would like to find in a treasure box.
Label the objects as well.

p

Read the following words to your student. If they hear a short sound "u" as in the word cub, then have them give a thumbs up. If they hear a long sound "u" as in cute, then have them give a thumbs down.

bug

bus

rug

cube

fume

mule

mug

nut

pup

tulip

unit

tub

tube

use

sun

run

Coin observations

Draw attention to the details on the front and back of coins with this money recognition activity. Provide students with a penny, nickel, dime, and quarter. Have students look at the coins as you ask them the following questions about each coin.

Who is the man on the coin?

What do the words on the coin say?

What is the building on the coin?

When was the coin made?

Does the coin have rough edges or smooth edges?

How much is a penny worth?

How much is a nickel worth?

How much is a dime worth?

How much is a quarter worth?

Practice initial sounds.  Look at this letter, what sound does it make?

Now draw five objects that begin with this letter that you would like to find in a treasure box. Label the objects as well.

q

Have students write the correct words under the beginning blends sound.

| bl | br | ch |
|---|---|---|
| cl | cr | dr |
| fl | fr | gl |

black          crab          glass          chain

clam

brag          dress          flag          free

This activity gives students practice with counting coins of the same denomination.  Give a handful of pennies and have child gently shake the handful of coins and then drop them on a carpet area.  Sort the coins based on the side that lands face up (heads or tails).

How many coins landed heads up?_____

How many coins landed tails up?_____

Now write a math problem to show how to add the above two numbers.

+_____

Practice initial sounds.  Look at this letter, what sound does it make?

Now draw five objects that begin with this letter that you would like to find in a treasure box. Label the objects as well.

r

Have students write the correct words under the beginning blends sound.

| gr | pl | pr |
|---|---|---|
| | | |
| sh | sl | sm |
| | | |
| st | th | wh |
| | | |

thin        small        slam        grab        plan

prize        sheep        stop        whale

Provide your student with a handful of coins. Let them choose coins to add up to the amount in each square.

| | |
|---|---|
| 5¢ | 15¢ |
| 25¢ | 30¢ |
| 50¢ | 8¢ |

Practice initial sounds.  Look at this letter, what sound does it make?

Now draw five objects that begin with this letter that you would like to find in a treasure box. Label the objects as well.

S

What's in your name?

Write each family member's name on this page and ask student's to try and find hidden words in the child's name.  For example:  ELIZABETH—bet, lit, hit, bat, at. Circle the person's name who had the most words formed from it.

Practice telling time.  Teach your child the hour times.

3:00          6:00          9:00

4:00          5:00          7:00

Practice initial sounds.  Look at this letter, what sound does it make?

Now draw five objects that begin with this letter that you would like to find in a treasure box. Label the objects as well.

t

# Word family houses

Fill in the word family houses with words that "live" inside.  For example: at: bat,cat, rat, sat, mat, fat

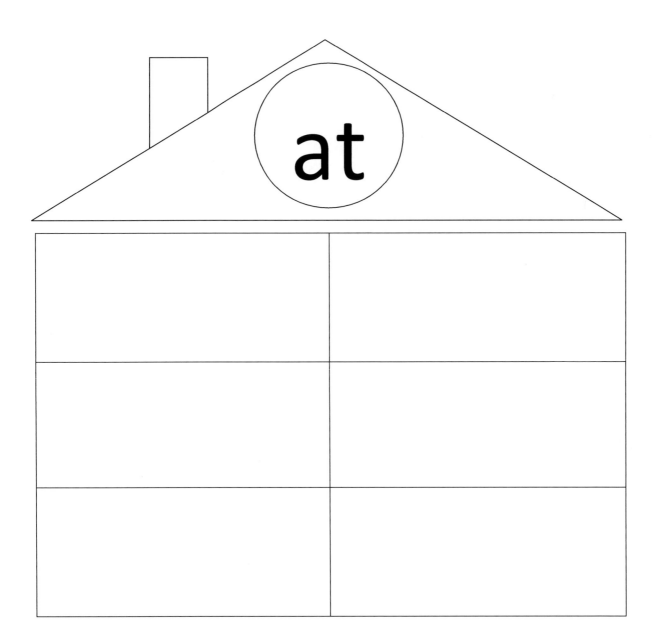

Have your child draw a related picture for each month of the year.  For example: January-snowman, February-hearts, etc.

| January | February | March |
|---|---|---|
| April | May | June |
| July | August | September |
| October | November | December |

Practice initial sounds.  Look at this letter, what sound does it make?

Now draw five objects that begin with this letter that you would like to find in a treasure box. Label the objects as well.

u

Fill in the word family houses with words that "live" inside.  For example: at: bat,cat, rat, sat,

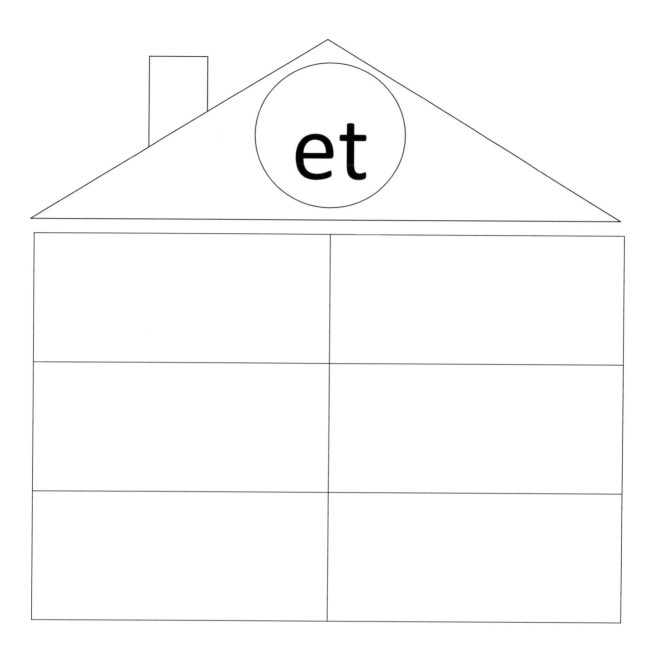

For this math activity take a piece of paper and cut it evenly into 4 sections. Write the numbers 1-4 on the squares. Do this on multiple pieces of paper up to the number 30  Place the squares on the floor in order, in a circle pattern  for your student.

Game suggestions:

- Call out a number and have them stand by it.
- Play some music and when the music stops, have them tell you which number they are standing on.
- Practice skip counting by stepping on every other number as they are calling them out loud.
- You can place them in a straight line and have them practice counting by 3's, 5's etc by stepping by the numbers.
- Play number mix up and put the numbers in a pile and let your child put them in the correct order.

Keep these numbers as they will do more activities another day.

Practice initial sounds.  Look at this letter, what sound does it make?

Now draw five objects that begin with this letter that you would like to find in a treasure box. Label the objects as well.

# V

Fill in the word family houses with words that "live" inside.  For example: at: bat,cat, rat, sat,

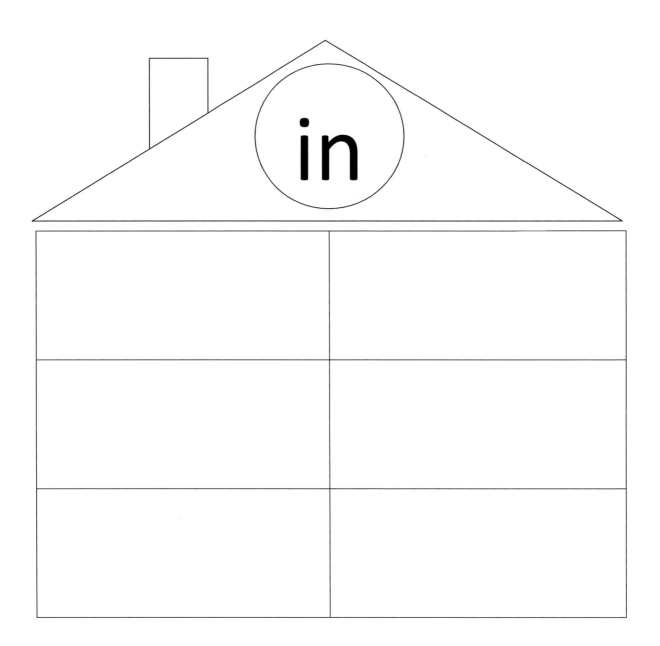

Even or odd?

Give each student some manipulative's or dried beans. Have the student count a corresponding number of manipulative's. To determine if the number is even or odd, have them separate them into groups of two. If the groups are equal in number, the number is even. If they are not equal and you have one left over, then it is odd.

| 5 | odd or even |
|---|---|
| 8 | odd or even |
| 12 | odd or even |
| 3 | odd or even |
| 13 | odd or even |

Practice initial sounds.  Look at this letter, what sound does it make?

Now draw five objects that begin with this letter that you would like to find in a treasure box. Label the objects as well.

W

Fill in the word family houses with words that "live" inside. For example: at: bat,cat, rat, sat.

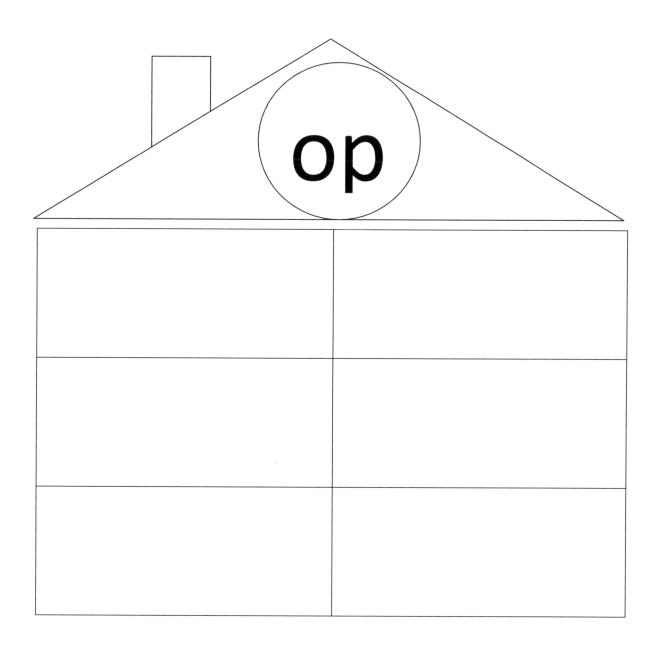

Copy the numbers from 1-10 and then make tally marks for each number.

| 1 | | |
| --- | --- | --- |
| 2 | | |
| 3 | | |
| 4 | | |
| 5 | | |
| 6 | | |
| 7 | | |
| 8 | | |
| 9 | | |
| 10 | | |

Practice initial sounds.  Look at this letter, what sound does it make?

Now draw five objects that begin with this letter that you would like to find in a treasure box. Label the objects as well.

X

Fill in the word family houses with words that "live" inside. For example: at: bat, cat, rat, sat,

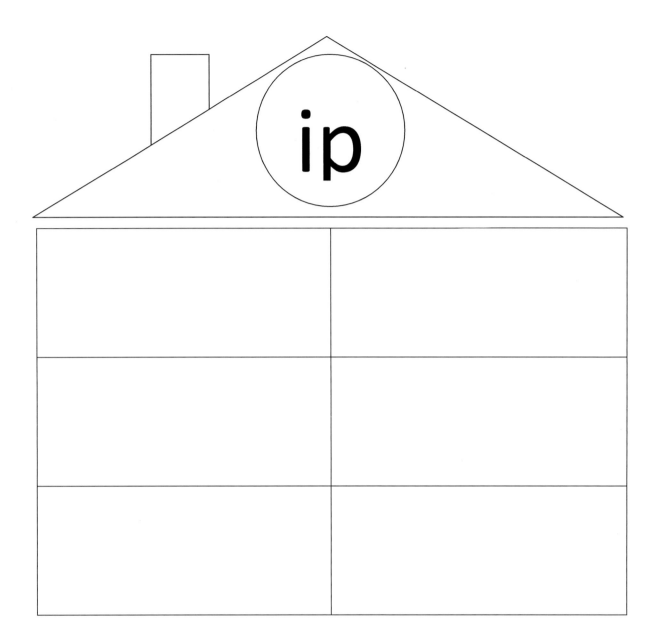

Starting from the left side.

Draw a smiley face on the second person.

Draw an angry face on the fifth person.

Draw a sad face on the first person.

Draw a surprised face on the third person.

Draw a face with glasses on the fourth person.

Practice initial sounds.  Look at this letter, what sound does it make?

Now draw five objects that begin with this letter that you would like to find in a treasure box. Label the objects as well.

Fill in the word family houses with words that "live" inside.  For example: at: bat,cat, rat, sat

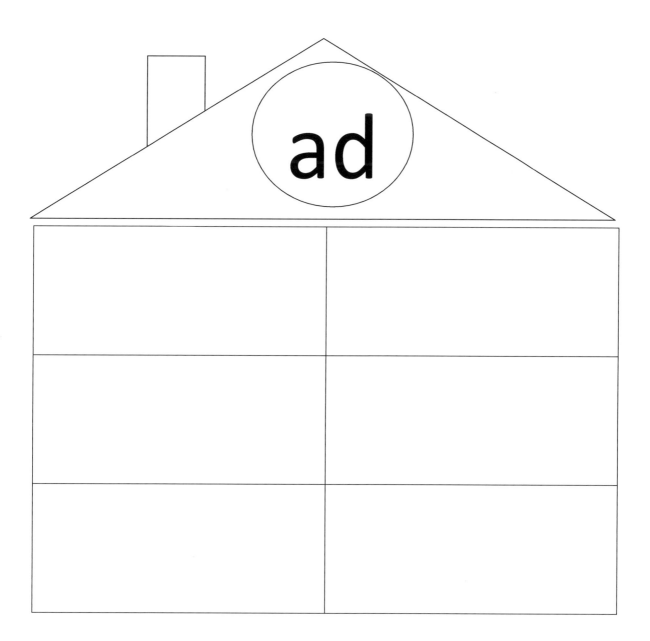

A handy tens and ones chart is just what you need to introduce place value. Distribute a supply of base ten rods and cubes to your student. To begin have students, place once cube at a time on the ones side of the chart until they can exchange ten cubes for one rod (to place on the tens side of the chart). Continue in this manner until your student has a good understanding of exchanging ten cubes for one rod. Save the cut outs to be used for future activities.(on the following page)

| tens 10s | ones 1s |
|---|---|
| | |

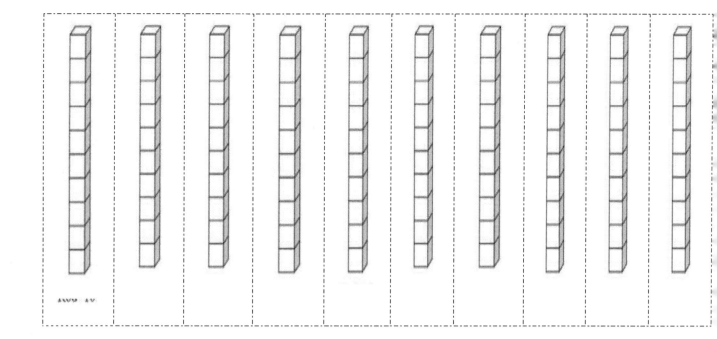

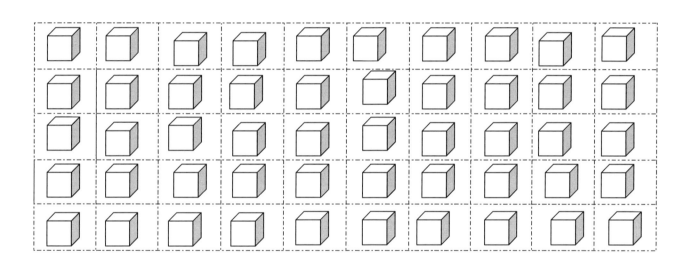

119

Left intentionally blank for the cut outs

Practice initial sounds.  Look at this letter, what sound does it make?

Now draw five objects that begin with this letter that you would like to find in a treasure box. Label the objects as well.

Z

Use the math manipulatives from yesterday for this activity.

Call out a number for your child and have them place the amount of rods and cubes to equal the number you call out.

| tens 10s | ones 1s |
|----------|---------|
|          |         |

Have your student add letters to the following rime.

_____ o c k      _____ o c k

_____ o c k      _____ o c k

_____ o c k      _____ o c k

_____ o c k      _____ o c k

Write your full name

_____

You are going to plant a garden.  Draw in the box what it would look like.

Let's write a story about what you would plant in your garden.

In my garden

Let's practice counting on the hundreds chart. Count out loud. Practice counting by 2's, 5's, 10's.

| 1 | 2 | 3 | 4 | 5 | 6 | 7 | 8 | 9 | 10 |
|---|---|---|---|---|---|---|---|---|----|
| 11 | 12 | 13 | 14 | 15 | 16 | 17 | 18 | 19 | 20 |
| 21 | 22 | 23 | 24 | 25 | 26 | 27 | 28 | 29 | 30 |
| 31 | 32 | 33 | 34 | 35 | 36 | 37 | 38 | 39 | 40 |
| 41 | 42 | 43 | 44 | 45 | 46 | 47 | 48 | 49 | 50 |
| 51 | 52 | 53 | 54 | 55 | 56 | 57 | 58 | 59 | 60 |
| 61 | 62 | 63 | 64 | 65 | 66 | 67 | 68 | 69 | 70 |
| 71 | 72 | 73 | 74 | 75 | 76 | 77 | 78 | 79 | 80 |
| 81 | 82 | 83 | 84 | 85 | 86 | 87 | 88 | 89 | 90 |
| 91 | 92 | 93 | 94 | 95 | 96 | 97 | 98 | 99 | 100 |

Add letters to the following rimes.

_____ eg     _____ an     _____ ip

_____ eg     _____ an     _____ ip

_____ eg     _____ an     _____ ip


_____ am     _____ en     _____ ot

_____ am     _____ en     _____ ot

_____ am     _____ en     _____ ot

Draw and color a picture of your animal in its habitat. Write the name of the animal on the line.

_____

1. My animal lives in _____.
2. My animal eats_____.
3. My animal moves with _____.
4. My animal's body is covered with_____.
5. Interesting facts about my animal:_____

_____

_____

Let's practice counting on the hundreds chart.  Count out loud. Practice counting by 2's, 5's, 10's.

| 1 | 2 | 3 | 4 | 5 | 6 | 7 | 8 | 9 | 10 |
|---|---|---|---|---|---|---|---|---|---|
| 11 | 12 | 13 | 14 | 15 | 16 | 17 | 18 | 19 | 20 |
| 21 | 22 | 23 | 24 | 25 | 26 | 27 | 28 | 29 | 30 |
| 31 | 32 | 33 | 34 | 35 | 36 | 37 | 38 | 39 | 40 |
| 41 | 42 | 43 | 44 | 45 | 46 | 47 | 48 | 49 | 50 |
| 51 | 52 | 53 | 54 | 55 | 56 | 57 | 58 | 59 | 60 |
| 61 | 62 | 63 | 64 | 65 | 66 | 67 | 68 | 69 | 70 |
| 71 | 72 | 73 | 74 | 75 | 76 | 77 | 78 | 79 | 80 |
| 81 | 82 | 83 | 84 | 85 | 86 | 87 | 88 | 89 | 90 |
| 91 | 92 | 93 | 94 | 95 | 96 | 97 | 98 | 99 | 100 |

# Plural practice

Singular means one and plural means more than one.

cat     dogs     bed     bats

singular                               plural

Draw a picture to depict the following:

| singular | plural |
| --- | --- |
|  |  |

Draw a picture of the things you found at the beach.  Then write a short story telling us what you found.

Circle the larger number:

32    21                     14        5

42    17                     33       32

11    7                      51       50

21    20                     77       78

Let's practice writing nouns.  Make a list of 10 nouns.  A noun names a person, place, or thing.

1. _____

2. _____

3. _____

4. _____

5. _____

6. _____

7. _____

8. _____

9. _____

10. _____

Let's make complete sentences with the following "mixed-up" word order.

jumped   in the library   Mr. Maryon

_____

ran   Ruby   down the street

_____

danced in the kitchen Mom

_____

Write your own complete sentence about your pet.

_____

Write your own complete sentence about the weather.

_____

3+2=                    1+1=

2+2=                    3+0=

4+1=                    5+1=

7+1=                    8+2=

3+3=                    5+5=

4+4=                    2+2=

# Descriptive Stuffed Animals

Draw a picture of your favorite stuffed animal.

Have your teacher write down a list of words that describe your favorite stuffed animal as you say them.

_____     _____          _____

_____     _____          _____

_____     _____          _____

Compound words

Finish each of the following to make compound words.

snow _____

cup _____

mail _____

foot _____

bath _____

bed _____

Can you think of three other compound words:

_____

_____

_____

Get two dice and roll 'em.

Here is a fun way for student's to improve recall of math facts. Have student's roll the dice and either add or subtract the two numbers. Then starting at the bottom of the recording sheet, have the student color in the correct box depicting the sum or difference rolled. Have student's continue in this same manner until they reach the top of one column. Have them announce which number reached the top first.

| 0 | 1 | 2 | 3 | 4 | 5 | 6 | 7 | 8 | 9 | 10 | 11 | 12 |
|---|---|---|---|---|---|---|---|---|---|----|----|----|
|   |   |   |   |   |   |   |   |   |   |    |    |    |
|   |   |   |   |   |   |   |   |   |   |    |    |    |
|   |   |   |   |   |   |   |   |   |   |    |    |    |
|   |   |   |   |   |   |   |   |   |   |    |    |    |
|   |   |   |   |   |   |   |   |   |   |    |    |    |
|   |   |   |   |   |   |   |   |   |   |    |    |    |

Write your full name on the line.  How many words can you find within your name?

_____

_____        _____

_____        _____

_____        _____

_____        _____

_____        _____

# Opposites

Fill in the following chart with magazine cut out images or drawn pictures to depict the opposite words show.

| big | little |
|-----|--------|
| **hot** | **cold** |

Get two dice and roll 'em.

Here is a fun way for student's to improve recall of math facts. Have student's roll the dice and either add or subtract the two numbers. Then starting at the bottom of the recording sheet, have the student color in the correct box depicting the sum or difference rolled. Have student's continue in this same manner until they reach the top of one column. Have them announce which number reached the top first.

| 0 | 1 | 2 | 3 | 4 | 5 | 6 | 7 | 8 | 9 | 10 | 11 | 12 |
|---|---|---|---|---|---|---|---|---|---|----|----|----|
|   |   |   |   |   |   |   |   |   |   |    |    |    |
|   |   |   |   |   |   |   |   |   |   |    |    |    |
|   |   |   |   |   |   |   |   |   |   |    |    |    |
|   |   |   |   |   |   |   |   |   |   |    |    |    |
|   |   |   |   |   |   |   |   |   |   |    |    |    |

Show your beginning readers how much they can already read with this challenge.  Place a supply of letter manipulatives and encourage them to create words.  When they create them, copy them on this page.  When they are finished, let them see all the words that they can read. This will boost their self-esteem.

# Words

# I

# Know

# Opposites

Fill in the following chart with magazine cut out images or drawn pictures to depict the opposite words show.

| Long | short |
|---|---|
| **In** | **out** |

Let's practice counting on the hundreds chart. Count out loud. Practice counting by 2's, 5's, 10's.

| 1 | 2 | 3 | 4 | 5 | 6 | 7 | 8 | 9 | 10 |
|---|---|---|---|---|---|---|---|---|-----|
| 11 | 12 | 13 | 14 | 15 | 16 | 17 | 18 | 19 | 20 |
| 21 | 22 | 23 | 24 | 25 | 26 | 27 | 28 | 29 | 30 |
| 31 | 32 | 33 | 34 | 35 | 36 | 37 | 38 | 39 | 40 |
| 41 | 42 | 43 | 44 | 45 | 46 | 47 | 48 | 49 | 50 |
| 51 | 52 | 53 | 54 | 55 | 56 | 57 | 58 | 59 | 60 |
| 61 | 62 | 63 | 64 | 65 | 66 | 67 | 68 | 69 | 70 |
| 71 | 72 | 73 | 74 | 75 | 76 | 77 | 78 | 79 | 80 |
| 81 | 82 | 83 | 84 | 85 | 86 | 87 | 88 | 89 | 90 |
| 91 | 92 | 93 | 94 | 95 | 96 | 97 | 98 | 99 | 100 |

# Sight word jumping

Copy the following sight words onto index cards and show them to your child one at a time. For every word they get correct, they get to jump one step closer to you. If you can't copy them, give them this list and let them read down the row. Have them do a jumping jack for every word they get correct. Work on the words they missed.

a

and

away

big

blue

can

come

down

find

for

funny

go

help

here

I

in

is

it

jump

little

Write words that rhyme with the first word in each row.

| | | |
|---|---|---|
| cat | | |
| sad | | |
| pot | | |
| red | | |
| man | | |
| log | | |

Let's practice counting on the hundreds chart. Count out loud. Practice counting by 2's, 5's, 10's.

| 1 | 2 | 3 | 4 | 5 | 6 | 7 | 8 | 9 | 10 |
|---|---|---|---|---|---|---|---|---|----|
| 11 | 12 | 13 | 14 | 15 | 16 | 17 | 18 | 19 | 20 |
| 21 | 22 | 23 | 24 | 25 | 26 | 27 | 28 | 29 | 30 |
| 31 | 32 | 33 | 34 | 35 | 36 | 37 | 38 | 39 | 40 |
| 41 | 42 | 43 | 44 | 45 | 46 | 47 | 48 | 49 | 50 |
| 51 | 52 | 53 | 54 | 55 | 56 | 57 | 58 | 59 | 60 |
| 61 | 62 | 63 | 64 | 65 | 66 | 67 | 68 | 69 | 70 |
| 71 | 72 | 73 | 74 | 75 | 76 | 77 | 78 | 79 | 80 |
| 81 | 82 | 83 | 84 | 85 | 86 | 87 | 88 | 89 | 90 |
| 91 | 92 | 93 | 94 | 95 | 96 | 97 | 98 | 99 | 100 |

# Sight word jumping

Copy the following sight words onto index cards and show them to your child one at a time. For every word they get correct, they get to jump one step closer to you. If you can't copy them, give them this list and let them read down the row. Have them do a jumping jack for every word they get correct. Work on the words they missed.

a

and

away

big

blue

can

come

down

find

for

funny

go

help

here

I

in

is

it

jump

little

A contraction is a short form of two words.  An apostrophe (') takes the place of the missing letters.  Can +not=can't

| didn't | can't | doesn't | isn't |

Write the contractions.

does not _____

did not _____

can not _____

is not _____

Write a sentence using a contraction from the box.

_____

## 2014
# April

| Sun | Mon | Tue | Wed | Thu | Fri | Sat |
|-----|-----|-----|-----|-----|-----|-----|
|     |     | 1   | 2   | 3   | 4   | 5   |
| 6   | 7   | 8   | 9   | 10  | 11  | 12  |
| 13  | 14  | 15  | 16  | 17  | 18  | 19  |
| 20  | 21  | 22  | 23  | 24  | 25  | 26  |
| 27  | 28  | 29  | 30  |     |     |     |

What day is April 3?_____

What days are the Sundays in April?_____

How many weeks are in April?_____

How many days are in April?_____

What day is April 28th?_____

A prediction is a guess about what will happen next. There are cookies on a plate. A good prediction would be that someone will eat the cookies.

Draw a line connecting each sentence with the one that tells what will happen next.

| | |
|---|---|
| Madelyn is late for school. | Jentzen will pick it up. |
| Autumn gets a doll. | The vet will help. |
| Dad gets a cake. | It will hop in. |
| A dog is sick. | She will run fast. |
| The frog sees a pond. | She will play with it. |
| The block falls down. | He eats it. |

Make your own prediction.

Stephen has a gift from his friend Paul.

_____

-  -  -  -  -  -  -  -  -  -  -  -  -  -  -  -  -  -  -  -  -  -  -  -

_____

# Sight word jumping

Copy the following sight words onto index cards and show them to your child one at a time. For every word they get correct, they get to jump one step closer to you. If you can't copy them, give them this list and let them read down the row. Have them do a jumping jack for every word they get correct. Work on the words they missed.

a

and

away

big

blue

can

come

down

find

for

funny

go

help

here

I

in

is

it

jump

little

Autumn likes cupcakes.  She had 8 cupcakes and Brooklyn gave her 3 more.  How many does she have?

Brooklyn had a pizza party.  She ordered 11 pizzas.  At the party they ate 6 of them.  How many does she have left?

Stephen raced his car around the track 6 times on Monday.  On Tuesday he raced it around 4 times.  How many times in all did he race around the track?

Jentzen loves legos.  He has 10 sets.  Stephen came and borrowed 3 of them.  How many does Jentzen have now?

ABC Order.

A library is organized in ABC order. It is much easier to find items when they are in alphabetical order. Let's practice putting the following in ABC order.

cat          apple          boy          dog

1 _____

2 _____

3 _____

4 _____

zebra          giraffe          monkey          elephant

1 _____

2 _____

3 _____

4 _____

# Sight word jumping-new list

Copy the following sight words onto index cards and show them to your child one at a time. For every word they get correct, they get to jump one step closer to you. If you can't copy them, give them this list and let them read down the row. Have them do a jumping jack for every word they get correct. Work on the words they missed.

look

make

me

my

not

one

play

red

sun

said

the

three

to

two

up

we

where

yellow

you

Grab a deck of cards and play WAR!

You will only need the number cards for this game.

Divide the cards among the number of players.

Keep the cards face down.

Each person flips up a card simultaneously.

The person with the highest card wins the "war".

If the cards are tied, they people who tied, flip another card to see who gets higher.

A syllable is a part of a word.

You can count the number of syllables in a word by counting the number of beats in the word.

Read the words below. Listen to the number of syllables in each word.

car=1          pump kin=2

Read each word. Circle the number of syllables in each word.

snack

1   2

basket

1   2

spin

1  2

under

1   2

stop

1   2

swim

1   2

wagon

1    2

spill

1   2

# Sight word jumping

Copy the following sight words onto index cards and show them to your child one at a time. For every word they get correct, they get to jump one step closer to you. If you can't copy them, give them this list and let them read down the row. Have them do a jumping jack for every word they get correct. Work on the words they missed.

look

make

me

my

not

one

play

red

sun

said

the

three

to

two

up

we

where

yellow

you

Grab a deck of cards and play WAR!

You will only need the number cards for this game.

Divide the cards among the number of players.

Keep the cards face down.

Each person flips up a card simultaneously.

The person with the highest card wins the "war".

If the cards are tied, they people who tied, flip another card to see who gets higher.

Circle the words that could describe the following:

**A firetruck**

Fast           soft           red

**A frog**

many          little         wet

**A sunshine**

black          one          hot

**A snowman**

three      big          hot

**Ants**

little          many         big

**Freshly baked cookies**

hot           stink         yum

# Sight word jumping

Copy the following sight words onto index cards and show them to your child one at a time.  For every word they get correct, they get to jump one step closer to you.  If you can't copy them, give them this list and let them read down the row.  Have them do a jumping jack for every word they get correct.  Work on the words they missed.

look

make

me

my

not

one

play

red

sun

said

the

three

to

two

up

we

where

yellow

you

# Math facts out loud

Read the following math facts to your child out loud and have them answer. If they learn best by moving---have them clap their hands every time they answer.  If they miss any, circle to work on it.

| | | |
|---|---|---|
| 0+0=0 | 0+1=1 | 0+2=2 |
| 1+0=1 | 1+1=2 | 1+2=3 |
| 2+0=2 | 2+1=3 | 2+2=4 |
| 3+0=3 | 3+1=4 | 3+2=5 |
| 4+0=4 | 4+1=5 | 4+2=6 |
| 5+0=5 | 5+1=6 | 5+2=7 |

Write the correct word in each sentence.

Jadyn slept in a _____.  tent/stop

A _____ is in the box.  sniff/snake

Do not _____ on the spill!  slip/sled

I like to _____ at the park.  swing/swat

A _____ is under the log.  slim/slug

Mom made a _____.  stem/list

# Sight word jumping-new list

Copy the following sight words onto index cards and show them to your child one at a time. For every word they get correct, they get to jump one step closer to you. If you can't copy them, give them this list and let them read down the row. Have them do a jumping jack for every word they get correct. Work on the words they missed.

all

am

are

at

ate

be

black

brown

but

came

did

do

eat

four

get

good

have

he

into

like

must

new

no

now

on

our

# Math facts out loud

Read the following math facts to your child out loud and have them answer. If they learn best by moving, have them clap their hands each time they answer.  If they miss any, circle to work on it.

| | | |
|---|---|---|
| 0+3=3 | 0+4=4 | 0+5=5 |
| 1+3=4 | 1+4=5 | 1+5=6 |
| 2+3=5 | 2+4=6 | 2+5=7 |
| 3+3=6 | 3+4=7 | 3+5=8 |
| 4+3=7 | 4+4=8 | 4+5=9 |
| 5+3=8 | 5+4=9 | 5+5=10 |

Fill in the following:

# My favorite list:

color:

food:

animal:

ice cream:

toy:

Practice writing your name.  Write your phone number.

# Sight word jumping

Copy the following sight words onto index cards and show them to your child one at a time. For every word they get correct, they get to jump one step closer to you. If you can't copy them, give them this list and let them read down the row. Have them do a jumping jack for every word they get correct. Work on the words they missed.

all

am

are

at

ate

be

black

brown

but

came

did

do

eat

four

get

good

have

he

into

like

must

new

no

now

on

our

Grab some change.  Teach your child the coins.  Show them how much they are worth.

Have them put the change on the chart to make the correct amount.

| | |
|---|---|
| 4¢ | |
| 25¢ | |
| 10¢ | |
| 21¢ | |
| 5¢ | |
| 7¢ | |
| 50¢ | |

Draw a picture of your favorite place. Write a sentence about why you like it.

My favorite place is

# Sight word jumping

Copy the following sight words onto index cards and show them to your child one at a time. For every word they get correct, they get to jump one step closer to you. If you can't copy them, give them this list and let them read down the row. Have them do a jumping jack for every word they get correct. Work on the words they missed.

all

am

are

at

ate

be

black

brown

but

came

did

do

eat

four

get

good

have

he

into

like

must

new

no

now

on

our

# Math facts out loud

Read the following math facts to your child out loud and have them answer. If they learn best by moving---have them clap their hands every time they answer.  If they miss any, circle to work on it.

| | | |
|---|---|---|
| 0+0=0 | 0+1=1 | 0+2=2 |
| 1+0=1 | 1+1=2 | 1+2=3 |
| 2+0=2 | 2+1=3 | 2+2=4 |
| 3+0=3 | 3+1=4 | 3+2=5 |
| 4+0=4 | 4+1=5 | 4+2=6 |
| 5+0=5 | 5+1=6 | 5+2=7 |

Circle the word in each group that names more than one.  Write it in the last box.

| | | | |
|---|---|---|---|
| watch | watches | what | |
| inches | pitch | inch | |
| such | lunch | lunches | |
| catch | patches | patch | |
| kisses | kiss | miss | |
| less | dresses | dress | |

# Sight word jumping-new list

Copy the following sight words onto index cards and show them to your child one at a time. For every word they get correct, they get to jump one step closer to you. If you can't copy them, give them this list and let them read down the row. Have them do a jumping jack for every word they get correct. Work on the words they missed.

out

please

pretty

ran

ride

saw

say

she

so

soon

that

there

they

this

too

under

want

was

well

went

what

white

who

will

with

yes

# Math facts out loud

Read the following math facts to your child out loud and have them answer. If they learn best by moving, have them clap their hands each time they answer. If they miss any, circle to work on it.

| | | |
|---|---|---|
| 0+3=3 | 0+4=4 | 0+5=5 |
| 1+3=4 | 1+4=5 | 1+5=6 |
| 2+3=5 | 2+4=6 | 2+5=7 |
| 3+3=6 | 3+4=7 | 3+5=8 |
| 4+3=7 | 4+4=8 | 4+5=9 |
| 5+3=8 | 5+4=9 | 5+5=10 |

Use the words in the box to answer the riddles.

| bike | hit | slide | slip | dig |
|------|-----|-------|------|-----|

You do this on the ice.  What word am I?

_____

You ride me fast up a hill. What word am I?

_____

You do this in the sand. What word am I?

_____

You do this with a bat in a game. What word am I?

_____

You like to race down me.  What word am I?

_____

# Sight word jumping-new list

Copy the following sight words onto index cards and show them to your child one at a time. For every word they get correct, they get to jump one step closer to you. If you can't copy them, give them this list and let them read down the row. Have them do a jumping jack for every word they get correct. Work on the words they missed.

out

please

pretty

ran

ride

saw

say

she

so

soon

that

there

they

this

too

under

want

was

well

went

what

white

who

will

with

yes

Get two dice and roll 'em.

Here is a fun way for student's to improve recall of math facts. Have student's roll the dice and either add or subtract the two numbers. Then starting at the bottom of the recording sheet, have the student color in the correct box depicting the sum or difference rolled. Have student's continue in this same manner until they reach the top of one column. Have them announce which number reached the top first.

| 0 | 1 | 2 | 3 | 4 | 5 | 6 | 7 | 8 | 9 | 10 | 11 | 12 |
|---|---|---|---|---|---|---|---|---|---|----|----|----|
|   |   |   |   |   |   |   |   |   |   |    |    |    |
|   |   |   |   |   |   |   |   |   |   |    |    |    |
|   |   |   |   |   |   |   |   |   |   |    |    |    |
|   |   |   |   |   |   |   |   |   |   |    |    |    |
|   |   |   |   |   |   |   |   |   |   |    |    |    |

Write the word that completes each sentence.

I can _____ the plum.

string   smell   shade

I would like a _____.

snack   scratch   snap

The _____ cat likes to play with string.

striped   scarf   steps

Boys and girls like to _____ in the water.

split   splash   scat

The _____ is hot!

sleet   strip   stove

Many people like the _____.

snap   split   spring

# Sight word jumping

Copy the following sight words onto index cards and show them to your child one at a time. For every word they get correct, they get to jump one step closer to you. If you can't copy them, give them this list and let them read down the row. Have them do a jumping jack for every word they get correct. Work on the words they missed.

out

please

pretty

ran

ride

saw

say

she

so

soon

that

there

they

this

too

under

want

was

well

went

what

white

who

will

with

yes

Let's practice counting on the hundreds chart.  Count out loud. Practice counting by 2's, 5's, 10's.

| 1 | 2 | 3 | 4 | 5 | 6 | 7 | 8 | 9 | 10 |
|---|---|---|---|---|---|---|---|---|---|
| 11 | 12 | 13 | 14 | 15 | 16 | 17 | 18 | 19 | 20 |
| 21 | 22 | 23 | 24 | 25 | 26 | 27 | 28 | 29 | 30 |
| 31 | 32 | 33 | 34 | 35 | 36 | 37 | 38 | 39 | 40 |
| 41 | 42 | 43 | 44 | 45 | 46 | 47 | 48 | 49 | 50 |
| 51 | 52 | 53 | 54 | 55 | 56 | 57 | 58 | 59 | 60 |
| 61 | 62 | 63 | 64 | 65 | 66 | 67 | 68 | 69 | 70 |
| 71 | 72 | 73 | 74 | 75 | 76 | 77 | 78 | 79 | 80 |
| 81 | 82 | 83 | 84 | 85 | 86 | 87 | 88 | 89 | 90 |
| 91 | 92 | 93 | 94 | 95 | 96 | 97 | 98 | 99 | 100 |

# Stop sign periods.

Your students will find that learning to use periods is a breeze with the help of stop signs. To prepare for this activity, cut four 1-inch octagons from red construction paper and write "STOP" on each cutout with a white crayon. Explain to your student that a period is similar to a stop sign. A stop sign tells a driver to stop. A period tells a reader to stop. A period signals the end of a complete thought and tells the reader to stop briefly before continuing. If a period is missing, the reader will not know to stop, and the words in one sentence will "crash" into another sentence.

After sharing this information with your student, read the following story to your student. Notice there isn't any periods. Challenge students to determine where the periods belong. Have them tape the stop signs in the correct places. Then invite them to join you as you reread the story this time pausing where the stop signs have been placed.

One day my dog and I went for a walk     We saw birds and cats We also saw a big black dog He scared us, so we went home

# Sight word jumping-new list

Copy the following sight words onto index cards and show them to your child one at a time. For every word they get correct, they get to jump one step closer to you. If you can't copy them, give them this list and let them read down the row. Have them do a jumping jack for every word they get correct. Work on the words they missed.

after
again
an
any
as
ask
by
could
every
fly
from
give
going
had
has
her
him
his
how
just
know

Lets learn how to write the words for numerals. Copy

1 one

2 two

3 three

4 four

5 five

6 six

7 seven

8 eight

9 nine

10 ten

Cross off the word that does not belong:

| | | |
|---|---|---|
| car | apple | purple |
| boat | pizza | white |
| ship | banana | circle |
| umbrella | orange | orange |

| | | |
|---|---|---|
| window | cat | tulip |
| door | hippo | tree |
| wall | dog | rose |
| cat | hamster | daffodil |

| | | |
|---|---|---|
| circle | 1 | s |
| square | m | n |
| frog | 5 | x |
| star | 4 | 2 |

| | | |
|---|---|---|
| mom | love | book |
| dad | heart | cd |
| sister | sweet | dvd |
| dog | anger | shelf |

# Sight word jumping

Copy the following sight words onto index cards and show them to your child one at a time. For every word they get correct, they get to jump one step closer to you. If you can't copy them, give them this list and let them read down the row. Have them do a jumping jack for every word they get correct. Work on the words they missed.

after

again

an

any

as

ask

by

could

every

fly

from

give

going

had

has

her

him

his

how

just

know

Cut out the hands of the clock and attach with a fastener.  Practice working with the hour and half hour times.

Intentionally left blank

Practice writing sentences correctly.

Sentences ALWAYS begin with a capital letter.

Sentences ALWAYS end with a punctuation mark.   ( ? . !)

Write each sentence correctly.  Add correct ending punctuation.

## the cat ate the mouse

## are you going to the park

## is it cold

## the dog barked at me

# Sight word jumping

Copy the following sight words onto index cards and show them to your child one at a time. For every word they get correct, they get to jump one step closer to you. If you can't copy them, give them this list and let them read down the row. Have them do a jumping jack for every word they get correct. Work on the words they missed.

after

again

an

any

as

ask

by

could

every

fly

from

give

going

had

has

her

him

his

how

just

know

Practice telling time with your student.

Practice counting on the 100's chart.

| 1 | 2 | 3 | 4 | 5 | 6 | 7 | 8 | 9 | 10 |
|---|---|---|---|---|---|---|---|---|---|
| 11 | 12 | 13 | 14 | 15 | 16 | 17 | 18 | 19 | 20 |
| 21 | 22 | 23 | 24 | 25 | 26 | 27 | 28 | 29 | 30 |
| 31 | 32 | 33 | 34 | 35 | 36 | 37 | 38 | 39 | 40 |
| 41 | 42 | 43 | 44 | 45 | 46 | 47 | 48 | 49 | 50 |
| 51 | 52 | 53 | 54 | 55 | 56 | 57 | 58 | 59 | 60 |
| 61 | 62 | 63 | 64 | 65 | 66 | 67 | 68 | 69 | 70 |
| 71 | 72 | 73 | 74 | 75 | 76 | 77 | 78 | 79 | 80 |
| 81 | 82 | 83 | 84 | 85 | 86 | 87 | 88 | 89 | 90 |
| 91 | 92 | 93 | 94 | 95 | 96 | 97 | 98 | 99 | 100 |

| | | |
|---|---|---|
| Draw 2 stars | Draw 1 circle | Draw 2 sad faces |
| Draw a square | Draw a star | Draw a red heart |
| Draw a yellow kite | Draw 3 horizontal lines | Draw 2 vertical lines |
| Draw a circle | Draw a pentagon | Draw a brown cat |
| Draw a black bear | Draw a tan cat | Draw 4 hearts |
| Draw a happy face | Draw a mad face | Draw a stick person |

# Sight word jumping

Copy the following sight words onto index cards and show them to your child one at a time. For every word they get correct, they get to jump one step closer to you. If you can't copy them, give them this list and let them read down the row. Have them do a jumping jack for every word they get correct. Work on the words they missed.

after
again
an
any
as
ask
by
could
every
fly
from
give
going
had
has
her
him
his
how
just
know

Practice telling time on the clock with your child.

Grab a deck of cards and play WAR!

You will only need the number cards for this game.

Divide the cards among the number of players.

Keep the cards face down.

Each person flips up a card simultaneously.

The person with the highest card wins the "war".

If the cards are tied, they people who tied, flip another card to see who gets higher.

Do you know the colors of the rainbow? ROY G BIV (red, orange, yellow, green, blue, indigo, violet).  Draw a rainbow with other outside pictures.

## What might you find at the end of the rainbow?

# Sight word jumping

Copy the following sight words onto index cards and show them to your child one at a time. For every word they get correct, they get to jump one step closer to you. If you can't copy them, give them this list and let them read down the row. Have them do a jumping jack for every word they get correct. Work on the words they missed.

after
again
an
any
as
ask
by
could
every
fly
from
give
going
had
has
her
him
his
how
just
know

Get two dice and roll 'em.

Here is a fun way for student's to improve recall of math facts. Have student's roll the dice and either add or subtract the two numbers. Then starting at the bottom of the recording sheet, have the student color in the correct box depicting the sum or difference rolled. Have student's continue in this same manner until they reach the top of one column. Have them announce which number reached the top first.

| | | | | | | | | | | | | |
|---|---|---|---|---|---|---|---|---|---|---|---|---|
| | | | | | | | | | | | | |
| | | | | | | | | | | | | |
| | | | | | | | | | | | | |
| | | | | | | | | | | | | |
| | | | | | | | | | | | | |
| 0 | 1 | 2 | 3 | 4 | 5 | 6 | 7 | 8 | 9 | 10 | 11 | 12 |

## Practice telling time with your student.

I fly around outside. I am yellow and black. I like to make honey. What insect am I?

I slither around on the ground. I have a long tongue. I make no noise. What am I?

I give milk to people. I am usually black and white. I like to eat grass out in the field. What animal am I?

I have 2 long ears. I hop around outside. I like to eat carrots. What am I?

I have a big trunk. I have large floppy ears. I suck up water in my trunk to throw on my back. What am I?

# Sight word jumping

Copy the following sight words onto index cards and show them to your child one at a time.  For every word they get correct, they get to jump one step closer to you.  If you can't copy them, give them this list and let them read down the row.  Have them do a jumping jack for every word they get correct.  Work on the words they missed.

after
again
an
any
as
ask
by
could
every
fly
from
give
going
had
has
her
him
his
how
just
know

## Hundred Board

| 1 | 2 | 3 | 4 | 5 | 6 | 7 | 8 | 9 | 10 |
|---|---|---|---|---|---|---|---|---|---|
| 11 | 12 | 13 | 14 | 15 | 16 | 17 | 18 | 19 | 20 |
| 21 | 22 | 23 | 24 | 25 | 26 | 27 | 28 | 29 | 30 |
| 31 | 32 | 33 | 34 | 35 | 36 | 37 | 38 | 39 | 40 |
| 41 | 42 | 43 | 44 | 45 | 46 | 47 | 48 | 49 | 50 |
| 51 | 52 | 53 | 54 | 55 | 56 | 57 | 58 | 59 | 60 |
| 61 | 62 | 63 | 64 | 65 | 66 | 67 | 68 | 69 | 70 |
| 71 | 72 | 73 | 74 | 75 | 76 | 77 | 78 | 79 | 80 |
| 81 | 82 | 83 | 84 | 85 | 86 | 87 | 88 | 89 | 90 |
| 91 | 92 | 93 | 94 | 95 | 96 | 97 | 98 | 99 | 100 |

Use the chart to help you answer.  Write the number that comes:

| Just before | Just after | between |
|---|---|---|
| _____43 | 49,_____ | 43,_____,45 |
| _____22 | 86,_____ | 21,_____,23 |
| _____99 | 19,_____ | 35,_____37 |

198

Cheese is to pizza as frosting is to:

hot dog                cupcakes                hamburgers

Lace is to shoe as zipper is to:

coat                sock                door

Socks are to feet as mittens are to:

arms                hands                dogs

Pink is to red as tan is to:

black                green                brown

# Sight word jumping-new list

Copy the following sight words onto index cards and show them to your child one at a time.  For every word they get correct, they get to jump one step closer to you.  If you can't copy them, give them this list and let them read down the row.  Have them do a jumping jack for every word they get correct.  Work on the words they missed.

let

live

may

of

old

once

open

over

put

round

some

stop

take

thank

them

then

think

walk

were

when

Let's practice filling in the hundreds chart.

| 1 | 2 | 3 | | 5 | 6 | | 8 | 9 | 10 |
|---|---|---|---|---|---|---|---|---|---|
| 11 | 12 | 13 | 14 | | 16 | 17 | | 19 | 20 |
| 21 | | | 24 | 25 | | 27 | 28 | 29 | |
| 31 | 32 | | 34 | | 36 | 37 | | 39 | |
| | 42 | 43 | | 45 | 46 | | 48 | 49 | 50 |
| | | 53 | 54 | 55 | 56 | 57 | 58 | | |
| 61 | | | 64 | 65 | | | 68 | | 70 |
| 71 | 72 | 73 | 74 | 75 | 76 | 77 | 78 | | 80 |
| | 82 | 83 | | | | 87 | 88 | 89 | 90 |
| 91 | 92 | 93 | 94 | 95 | 96 | | | | 100 |

Read on your own and answer the following questions:

Can you pet a cat?     yes or  no

Can you ride a bike?    yes or no

Is a frog green?        yes or no

Are you taller than a flower?      yes or no

Are you heavier than an elephant?      yes or no

Can you eat a tree?            yes or no

Is the sun in the water?    yes or no

Is the clouds on the ground?   yes or no

Can you count up to ten?            yes or no

Do you like to eat ants?       yes or no

Do you like to play with lions?            yes or no

# Sight word jumping

Copy the following sight words onto index cards and show them to your child one at a time.  For every word they get correct, they get to jump one step closer to you.  If you can't copy them, give them this list and let them read down the row.  Have them do a jumping jack for every word they get correct.  Work on the words they missed.

let

live

may

of

old

once

open

over

put

round

some

stop

take

thank

them

then

think

walk

were

when

# Math facts out loud

Read the following math facts to your child out loud and have them answer. If they learn best by moving---have them clap their hands every time they answer. If they miss any, circle to work on it.

| | | |
|---|---|---|
| 0+0=0 | 0+1=1 | 0+2=2 |
| 1+0=1 | 1+1=2 | 1+2=3 |
| 2+0=2 | 2+1=3 | 2+2=4 |
| 3+0=3 | 3+1=4 | 3+2=5 |
| 4+0=4 | 4+1=5 | 4+2=6 |
| 5+0=5 | 5+1=6 | 5+2=7 |

Where would you find the following in your home:

milk _____

books_____

ice cream_____

spoons_____

shoes_____

crayons_____

What might you find inside:

coat pocket_____

purse_____

drawer_____

# Sight word jumping

Copy the following sight words onto index cards and show them to your child one at a time. For every word they get correct, they get to jump one step closer to you. If you can't copy them, give them this list and let them read down the row. Have them do a jumping jack for every word they get correct. Work on the words they missed.

let

live

may

of

old

once

open

over

put

round

some

stop

take

thank

them

then

think

walk

were

when

# Math facts out loud

Read the following math facts to your child out loud and have them answer. If they learn best by moving, have them clap their hands each time they answer. If they miss any, circle to work on it.

| | | |
|---|---|---|
| 0+3=3 | 0+4=4 | 0+5=5 |
| 1+3=4 | 1+4=5 | 1+5=6 |
| 2+3=5 | 2+4=6 | 2+5=7 |
| 3+3=6 | 3+4=7 | 3+5=8 |
| 4+3=7 | 4+4=8 | 4+5=9 |
| 5+3=8 | 5+4=9 | 5+5=10 |

# What is their profession?

I work on cars keeping them running. If your brakes go out, I am the person to call. Who am I?

If you are in an accident and you need immediate care, they bring you to me and I can perform surgery to help fix you. Who am I?

I make pastries and all kinds of cakes and pies. Who am I?

After you leave your hotel room, I come and clean it up for you. Who am I?

I work at your local church. If you have a need or just someone to talk to, I am here. I do my preaching on Sunday. Who am I?

I put out fires or any type of rescue needs. Who am I?

# Sight word jumping

Copy the following sight words onto index cards and show them to your child one at a time. For every word they get correct, they get to jump one step closer to you. If you can't copy them, give them this list and let them read down the row. Have them do a jumping jack for every word they get correct. Work on the words they missed.

let

live

may

of

old

once

open

over

put

round

some

stop

take

thank

them

then

think

walk

were

when

# Draw a line to the correct time.

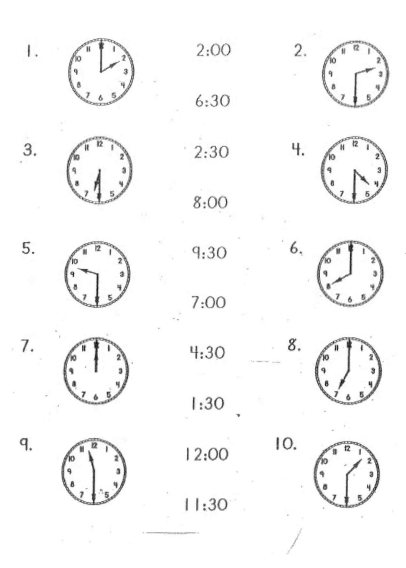

1.

2:00

6:30

2.

3.

2:30

8:00

4.

5.

9:30

7:00

6.

7.

4:30

1:30

8.

9.

12:00

11:30

10.

Sort the words into two groups.

| | | | | |
|---|---|---|---|---|
| cow | girls | children | bear | men |
| frog | mother | snake | bird | boys |

## People

## Animals

# Sight word jumping

Copy the following sight words onto index cards and show them to your child one at a time. For every word they get correct, they get to jump one step closer to you. If you can't copy them, give them this list and let them read down the row. Have them do a jumping jack for every word they get correct. Work on the words they missed.

let
live
may
of
old
once
open
over
put
round
some
stop
take
thank
them
then
think
walk
were
when

Fill in the calendar dates. Then answer the questions on the lines provided. This month has 31 days. The first day of the month is Monday.

## December

| Sunday | Monday | Tuesday | Wednesday | Thursday | Friday | Saturday |
|--------|--------|---------|-----------|----------|--------|----------|
|        |        |         |           |          |        |          |
|        |        |         |           |          |        |          |
|        |        |         |           |          |        |          |
|        |        |         |           |          |        |          |
|        |        |         |           |          |        |          |

1. What day of the week is December 4?_____

2. How any Wednesdays are in December?_____

3. What day of the week is December 20?_____

4. How many Fridays are in December?_____

5. What day of the week is December 31?_____

Let's practice your writing before the school year begins.  Use your neatest handwriting and copy the letters correctly three times each.

a

b

c

d

e

f

g

h

i

j

k

l

m

n

o

p

q

r

s

t

u

v

w

x

y

z

Practice and review any of your reading sight word lists from this book. Go over your cards of any that were challenging.

# Additional math practice

Teach your student the months of the year. ☐

Teach your student the days of the week ☐

Be able to count up to 100. ☐

Have your student write the numbers 1-20 below ☐

Noun= names a person, place, or thing
Verb=something you do; action word

Write N beside the word if it is a noun.
Write V beside the word if it is a verb.


pig  _____          sit  _____

run  _____          hop _____

boat_____          room _____

sleep_____          paper_____

seal _____          yell _____

sack _____          play _____

book_____          car  _____

Let's practice your writing before the school year begins. Use your neatest handwriting and copy the letters correctly three times each.

a

b

c

d

e

f

g

h

i

j

k

l

m

n

o

p

q

r

s

t

u

v

w

x

y

z

Made in the USA
Columbia, SC
31 March 2021